Pamelot

Mr Unk

Zig and Zag

Queen Pamela

Wizard Klang

Lord Tim

Viktor the Bad

Dragonville! The best spot in the Kingdom of Pamelot!

Hooray! We love Queen Pam! She is a star! And hooray for Lord Tim!

Hooray!

Yes, things in Dragonville were better than they had ever been.

Unless, you were one of the Unks ...

The Unks did not live in a grand house. They lived in a hut in Slug Swamp.

Mr Unk and his twins, Zig and Zag, were Dragonville's pest controllers.

Zig was cooking supper. Boiled twig and turnip slop. Zig's twin, Zag, was hunting frogs.

Come on, Zig! We are playing Hunt The Frog! Then Dad is going to let us see the boil on his ear!

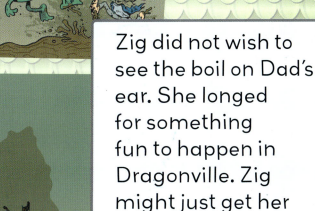

Zig did not wish to see the boil on Dad's ear. She longed for something fun to happen in Dragonville. Zig might just get her wish. Very soon.

The next day, Zig and Zag were in the tunnels under Dragonville Castle.

What is that smell? How come Dad sends *us* on the jobs that smell?

What smell? He said he has got important stuff to do at the market.

Yes, I bet.

Unk Pest Control

You hear that, Zag?

Skig... Skag... Skrag...

I do not like the look of this!

What can we do, Zag?

Grrrrr!

Zag?

RUN!

Craaaaark!

6

A dragon?

Yes.
A dragon.
I saw it! I did!

It was big!
There was fire
and stuff!

Rubbish! There
are no dragons in
Dragonville! Lord Tim
and his knights got
rid of them years ago!

But we tell
the town
we get rid of
dragons! It
says so on
the cart!

We can get
rid of dragons!

If there were some.

Which there
are not.

Zig had a clever way to get into the castle.

Will this work, Zig?

Yes! No problem! Fingers crossed.

Zig's path into the castle led them under the Red Trolls. Zig had been here with Dad last year.

This way! Shh! The Red Trolls are just there!

Keep going, Zag!

Zig and Zag padded past the Pup of Terror.

And slid past Sid the Small.

This is it!

Is Queen Pamela in there?

Let me see.

I can tell you how I got rid of the dragons, Queen Pam!

No, thank you, Lord Tim. But you can get me a unicorn.

15

Zag pushed Zig out of the way.

The door crashed open!

The door opened. Zig and Zag fell into the Hall of Pamelot! And landed on Queen Pam.

Wait! Wait! We are Zig and Zag from Unk Pest Control! We have something big to report, Your Majesty!

What could you pests have to say to Queen Pam? Be quick!

There is something under the castle! Something big! Something horrid!

What rot!

Perhaps we could let them tell us what they saw, Your Majesty?

Very well. What do you think is under the castle?

A dragon.

19

Um. Ah. Yes. Thank you, Klang. Thing is, you see, I—

You said you had kicked all the dragons out of Dragonville, Lord Tim.

That is right!

And I got rid of them! So there are NO dragons under the castle!

But I will get you a unicorn, Your Majesty! A rainbow one!

Unicorns?

A rainbow unicorn! You are my best knight, Lord Tim!

What about the little pests, Your Majesty?

Oh, them. Lock them up for a year or so, Viktor. Put their dad in, too!

Unicorns! Skweeeeee!

Lord Tim and his knights set out on the hunt for Queen Pam's rainbow unicorn.

Do you need to have all the knights with you, Lord Tim? It seems a lot for one little unicorn.

The Unks did say there was a dragon out there. Like to stay and help?

Must dash! Rainbow unicorns are very hard to track down, Your Majesty! Bye-eee!

Three nights after Lord Tim left ...

Did you hear that?

Huh?

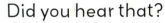

Craaaaarrk!

Woah!

A noise shook the castle from top to bottom.

All the knights were looking for rainbow unicorns.
Dragonville Castle was helpless!

And then ...

Freedom!

Klang was the best wizard in all of Pamelot. But there was something he had never confessed. His magic tricks never worked!

Quick, Klang! Turn the dragon into a turnip or something!

I will have a go, Your Majesty.

What can we do, Zig?

We are Dragonville's pest controllers! We have to do something!

Yum!

Handbagius Maximus Instanto! Handbag now! Dragonus Baggus!

The dragon will scoff him!

29

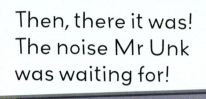

As the sun began to come up, the Unks set off back to Slug Swamp.

No more dragons in Dragonville!

I wonder how Lord Tim's unicorn hunt is going?

The unicorn hunt was not going well.

Forgive me, Rainbow Unicorn Dragon! Do not munch me up! I did think you might be smaller!

Chat about the book

1 Go to page 5. What were Zig and Zag doing?

2 Look at page 16. The door crashed open. Why did this happen?

3 Look at page 22. What did Mr Unk think about the prison at Dragonville Castle?

4 Look at page 25. Dragonville Castle was helpless. Explain what 'helpless' tells us.

5 The unicorn hunt at the end of the story was not going well for Lord Tim. What do you think will happen next?

6 This book is like a comic. Do you like comics? Explain why or why not.

DRAGONVILLE
The Unks of Slug Swamp

Written by Martin Chatterton

Illustrated by Martin and Annie Chatterton

ISBN: 9781398324336

Text © 2021 Martin Chatterton
Illustrations, design and layout © Hodder and Stoughton Ltd
First published in 2021 by Hodder & Stoughton Limited (for its Rising Stars imprint, part of the Hodder Education Group),
An Hachette UK Company
Carmelite House, 50 Victoria Embankment, London EC4Y 0DZ

www.risingstars-uk.com

Impression number 10 9 8 7 6 5 4 3 2 1
Year 2025 2024 2023 2022 2021

Author and illustrator: Martin Chatterton
Series Editor: Tony Bradman
Commissioning Editor: Hamish Baxter
Educational Reviewer: Helen Marron
Joint Illustrator: Annie Chatterton
Design and page layout: Helen Townson
Editor: Amy Tyrer

With thanks to the schools that took part in the development of Reading Planet KS2, including: Ancaster CE Primary School, Ancaster; Downsway Primary School, Reading; Ferry Lane Primary School, London; Foxborough Primary School, Slough; Griffin Park Primary School, Blackburn; St Barnabas CE First & Middle School, Pershore; Tranmoor Primary School, Doncaster; and Wilton CE Primary School, Wilton.

A catalogue record for this title is available from the British Library.

Printed in India.

Orders: Please contact Hachette UK Distribution, Hely Hutchinson Centre, Milton Road, Didcot, Oxfordshire, OX11 7HH.
Telephone: (44) 01235 400555. Email: primary@hachette.co.uk

MIX
Paper from
responsible sources
FSC™ C104740
www.fsc.org